The Truth About
Dungeons & Dragons

JOAN HAKE ROBIE

▲

The Truth About

Dungeons & Dragons

JOAN HAKE ROBIE

P.O. Box 4123, Lancaster, Pennsylvania 17604

JOAN HAKE ROBIE is author of thirteen books, which include *Halloween And Satanism, Turmoil In The Toy Box II,* and *Teenage Mutant Ninja Turtles Exposed!* Joan has appeared on TV shows such as Geraldo Rivera, Sonja Live, 9 Broadcast Plaza, and Heritage Today. Joan conducts seminars throughout· the country bringing up-to-date information on the toy and cartoon industry, the occult, and other timely subjects.

To schedule Author appearances write: Author Appearances, Starburst Promotions, P.O. Box 4123, Lancaster, PA 17604 or call (717)-293-0939.

Credits:

Cover Art by Dave Ivey.

THE TRUTH ABOUT DUNGEONS AND DRAGONS
Copyright ©1991 by Starburst, Inc.
All rights reserved.

First Printing, November 1991

ISBN: 0-914984-37-3
Library of Congress Catalog Number 91-66238

Printed in the United States of America

Dedication

To all the gifted young men and women who are involved in the role-playing game of *Dungeons & Dragons*. May your eyes be opened to the truth.

Contents

Preface

People everywhere (young and old) are searching for truth. Some are looking to New Age philosophies, others are turning to what they call the "old religion"—paganism, which is in reality witchcraft and Satanism. Some turn to role-playing games like *Dungeons and Dragons*.

Who plays *Dungeons and Dragons*? The typical role-playing gamer is a teenaged white male from a middle class background. He is bright, analytical and tireless. He is above average in intelligence and interested in math and science.

One young man named Sean, who is in prison for killing his mother and father, admits that *Dungeons and Dragons* played a key role in opening him up to the demonic realm.

Being the mother of grown sons who are bright, analytical, and tireless (to my knowledge they have never played *Dungeons and Dragons*), I have concern for all the gifted young men (and women) who are caught in the clutches of the game of *Dungeons and Dragons*.

If you, or anyone you know, are involved in this deadly game, you need to read this book.

1

Fantasy Versus Reality

That wonderful world of "let's pretend" is being influenced today in a way that researchers never really considered a danger. Too much time spent in the imaginary world affects all ages, disorienting the way they view reality. **Psychologists have claimed, time and again, that when someone lives in the realm of fantasy for an extended length of time, the lines dividing reality and fantasy become distorted, fuzzy.**

In the last decade, this concept has been proven to be a real and increasing danger. The contributing force behind it for many youths has been *Dungeons and Dragons* and other fantasy role-playing games. *Dungeons and Dragons* can be described as follows:

- The bizarre cast list of characters includes demons, dragons, witches, zombies, harpies, gnomes, and creatures who cast spells and exercise supernatural powers.
- It dabbles with demonic spirits and promotes the influence of the occult.
- It encourages sex and violence
- It is a form of Devil worship.
- It has been banned from the public schools in Utah, summer recreational programs in California, and a minister in Kansas wants to collect money to purchase and burn every copy he can find.

The controversy surrounding *Dungeons and Dragons* continues as does the popularity of this anti-religious role-playing game that encourages players to fantasize forbidden temptations of the civilized world. Bloodshed, mayhem, and murder are common events as players "pretend" to pillage, rape, and cast magic spells in their quest for riches, knowledge, and superhuman powers. This is a game of human violence that features occult practices such as magic, sorcery, divination, casting spells, and having "powers" over others, especially demons. Many of the spells and magic used are described in books of witchcraft. At the very least, *Dungeons and Dragons* is an obsessive retreat from reality. As I said before, psychologists have claimed, again and again, that when someone lives in the realm of fantasy for an extended period of time, the lines dividing reality and fantasy become distorted or fuzzy. This is a real and increasing danger. One *Dungeons and Dragons* (commonly referred to as *D & D*) player is quoted: "The more I play *D & D*, the more I want to get away from this world. The whole thing is getting very bad."[1]

Unlike the other board games, *Dungeons and Dragons* becomes a compulsive force in the lives of those who play it. *D & D* requires each player to make philosophical, religious and moral decisions, whereas ordinary games do not. Eventually, the more a player participates in the game, the more he chooses to remain in the fantasy world, and the harder it will be for him to accept his responsibilites in the real world. The makeup of the game lends itself to an undisciplined overindulgence as creator Gary Gygax says, "You have to pursue *D & D* with your whole soul if you're going to do well at it." When doing this "pursuing the game with his whole soul," a player often has trouble differentiating between the game and reality.

We must recognize the dangers of our children spending so much time playing this game. It often leads to a distortion of reality, as well as filling the child's mind with images of the occult.

2

What Is
Dungeons & Dragons?

The game *Dungeons and Dragons* is a tremendously gripping fantasy role-playing game. Its players seek to build up personal power. They penetrate a "Dungeon," a maze, city or world created in the mind of the Dungeon Master who is the key person in the game. Players battle supernatural beings, monsters from antiquity, and creatures from other worlds in order to seize hidden treasures.

The game and its derivatives have been popular for over fifteen years. Tactical Studies Rules Association, the manufacturer of *D & D* and its accessories mounted a renewed advertising campaign in 1989 and released several new products. *Advanced Dungeons and Dragons* has been released in a second edition. It is billed as having "all new monsters" described in a three volume *Monstrous Compen-*

dium available for Christmas gift-giving. Also available is *Dungeon*. According to magazine advertisements, this game for eight-year-olds offers:

> **A romp 'em, stomp 'em roaring good time of monsterbashing, dungeon crawling and treasure collecting for the entire family! Dwarf, elf, warrior, magic-user, cleric and fighter—one, any, or all— enter the depths of a dungeon notorious for the ferocity of its monsters and the hoards of treasure stored within its dank walls.**[2]

TSR has supported their products with comprehensive, aggressive advertising campaigns and promotions. Their products appear inside every issue of DC and Marvel Comics which reach 40 million readers each month. In addition, TSR is licensing out many of its key products to become a line of comics and computer game software.

Where most games have a 3-year life cycle, *D & D* is over 15 years old and still in the top 10. About one million people, both in the United States and abroad, play *Dungeons and Dragons* according to E. Gary Gygax, president of the company that produces it. The basic set, introduced in 1974 begins with a 63-page players' manual and a 48-page rule book. Players are given background information on monsters, magic spells and treasures.

D & D is extremely complicated and time-consuming. One player, the *Dungeon Master*, runs the game. He maps out on paper his own elaborate maze of rooms and corridors filled with monsters, traps, magic items, guardians, and treasure. The Dungeon Master, is a referee, diecaster, and all-around god, an "all-knowing and all-seeing emcee," said *Life Magazine*.[3] He is the most powerful person in the universe. His chief sources are Greek mythology and medieval history. Other players have no idea what is waiting for them when they assume the role of a specific character who has special abilities.

D & D is a game that takes place almost entirely within the minds of its players. There are no cards, no boards, no play money. Each player, with the exception of the omnipotent "DM," as the Dungeon Master is called, determines his abilities in such areas as strength, intelligence, and charisma by rolling dice. Each chooses a race (elfin, dwarfin, etc.), profession (fighter, magic user, thief, etc.) and moral alignment (from lawful good to chaotic evil). Each player chooses a physical shape, from human to elf, dwarf, gnome, or half orc, and a basic role (druid, cleric, fighter, or magic user). Players can arm their characters with a variety of ominous weapons such as daggers, hand axes, swords, and battle axes. They are also equipped with special aids to survive their journey through the dungeons: magical weapons, potions, spells and magical trinkets such as holy water, garlic, and wolfsbane. The personalities of the characters turn out to be combinations of people's idealized alter egos and their less-than-ideal impulses. Another dice roll determines "hit points," the amount of physical punishment a character can endure without dying. Roll of dice determines starting cash.

Players are motivated almost entirely by greed as the characters ban together to fight their way through the monster-laden maze, grabbing as much treasure as they can while the DM rolls the dice to determine what horrors they will encounter. The DM's scenario is studded with forbidding obstacles. The player may have to fend off attacks from rapacious bands of gnomes, screeching harpies, and vicious wererats, or he may be stymied by paralyzing Gray Ooze. The success of his journey depends on his assigned skills and the judgement of the DM.

Players use a map and miniature figures to plot their course, keeping track of details on graph paper, but the game is largely in the minds of the players. The Dungeon Master creates a dramatic situation. It usually consists of a set of maps that carefully notes every trap, treasure, monster, and magical device the heroes of the story are likely to find. Charms or magic spells are often used by players or the DM and can be resisted. The player rolls two dice that are read as a percentage to see if the event did occur—called a "saving throw." If the dice come up at a lower percentage, the character is saved from the spell. A game can go on for years. Rolls of the dice determine much of the action, but the game is loaded with options. This is another part of *D & D*'s appeal. However, players have been devastated to the point of suicidal depression when a wrong decision on their part led to the death of a character with whom they equated closely. *Dungeons and Dragons* is a complicated game with elaborate rule books, endless note-taking, map-drawing, probability charts and oddly shaped dice.

The DM plays the parts of all the bad guys and monsters while players decide the character's actions. Combat and magic are resolved by the roll of the dice. At the end of the game the characters are awarded any earned treasure, and an increment of "experience" which elevates them toward still more superhuman powers.

Characters carry to their next game previously acquired possessions and experience, each player following his character's career through until death.

3

The Creator
And The Creation

"Do you have Gygax's autograph?" a teenager was overheard to ask. "I'll give you $100. How about $150? The man is a genius. When he wrote the rules for *D & D*, his hand was guided."

Inveterate game players tend to say things like this about the man they call "The Creator." Gary Gygax is the most visible of the men behind the role-playing games. "He has been dubbed 'the darling of the game industry,' basking in his role as a cult figure . . . . He is also the man some people equate with the devil."

Gary Gygax was a bored insurance underwriter and inveterate games player who had mastered chess at the age of six. As an adolescent he spent his allowance on miniature metal soldiers and staged battlefield maneuvers. He loved

19

games and the myths and fairy tales told him by his father. He became a war game aficionado as a college student during the 1960's and was part of a group that met on weekends to reenact historic battles using miniature figures. His particular passion became writing war games for toy soldiers, just as H.G. Wells had done. One day Gygax dreamed up and wrote down a sort of war game not confined to historical reality at all, but rather a mythic fantasy game that would draw on his extensive reading of such books as *Arms and Armor*, the *Welsh Wars of Edward I*, and much fantasy fiction. He called it *Dungeons and Dragons*. It was rejected by two game companies, including Avalon Hill (the king of the wargames) who said it was too complicated and open-ended.

If Gygax had not lost his insurance job, that might have been the end of *D & D*. Losing his job shocked him into asking himself what he really wanted to do with his life. The answer was to earn a living from creating games. He has since applied the role-playing, probability-balancing game concept to espionage in a game called Top Secret, to science fiction in Gamma World and the Wild West in Boot Hill.

Gygax began to see weak spots in the sales appeal of *D & D*. One was the amount of time it took to prepare for a game—four or five hours, much of it spent creating a "dungeon." Another drawback was that many potential players needed to have their imaginations stimulated. As a result, Gygax employed his rich inner fantasy life and imagination to package ready-made fantasy dungeon settings called "modules" with names such as Vault of the Drow and Glacial Rift of the Frost Giant Jarl. The *Dungeon Master's Guide*, the *Players Handbook*, and lavishly illustrated *Monster Manual* and *Gods, Demigods and Heroes* found a ready-made audience.[4]

In the works by 1980 was a simplified version of the board game for younger players, an electronic game, and a movie.

The Business Of *D & D*

The Tactical Studies Rules Association was founded by Gary Gygax and Don Kaye in 1973 with a total investment of $1,000. The game was first marketed in 1974 after Flint Dille became a partner. It took nearly a year for Gygax to sell the first 1,000 official copies of *D & D* printed that year, but the second 2,000 booklet order disappeared in just five months. In 1975, Brian Bloom, also an inveterate gamesman, joined as an investor and they incorporated as TSR Hobbies Inc.

Financial problems, due to meteoric expansion, forced TSR Hobbies to turn to Flint Dille's sister, Lorraine Williams, who bought Bloom's interest in the company. By 1978 sales had hit $2.2 million and grossed $20 million in 1980. Gygax put most of his earnings back into the company and saw revenues multiply more than ten-fold by 1982. By this time, the game was selling at a rate of 1,000 per month.[5]

The combination of Gygax and Williams didn't work out, and in 1986 they split and formed two new companies. Williams remained the Chief Executive Officer of TSR, Inc., and Gygax formed New Infinities Productions, Inc.

The role-playing games turned into books about 6 years ago and now both TSR, Inc. and New Infinities Productions are turning out more books than games. TSR, Inc. also publishes *The Dragon*, a $3 monthly magazine with a circulation of 10,000.

4

Where Do The
Monsters Come From?

The manticore is a huge lion-bodied monstrosity with a human face, dragon wings, and a tail full of iron spikes. The twenty-four spikes can be fired, six at a time, like crossbow bolts with a 180-foot range. Their favorite prey is man.

Sounds dreadful, doesn't it? However, even a manticore takes a backseat to a dragon, of which there are four different species: white, black, red, and brass. Brass is the worst. All dragons breathe fire and spew sleep, magic, and fear all over the place. Being intelligent creatures, they can be negotiated with on occasion, and the older they are, the more treasure they conceal.

The world of *D & D* is based on the legends, fairy tales and literature of Western Europe, with a scattering on items from other cultures. To some extent, it resembles the Middle Earth of JRR Tolkien's grand epic, *Lord of the Rings*, or the novels of H.G. Wells. Gygax compares it to a boom town in the Alaskan gold rush. The value of everything is inflated, money is cheap, adventurers are bringing gold and jewels out of the dungeons by the bucketful and magical items abound. It is like the perilous Africa of H. Rider Haggard, the ancient Hyperborean world of Robert E. Howard's *Conan*, or the magic ridden universe of Fritz Leiber's *Farfred and the Grey Mouser.*

The rules of *D & D* conform to a common background of myth and fairy tales. It is a medieval world, one without modern technology or gunpowder, but one with compensatory magic as the technology. Telepathy replaces radio, the crystal ball replaces television, and the fire-ball spell takes the place of the cannon and the machine gun.

Dr. Gary North, author of *None Dare Call It Witchcraft* has a lot to say about *Dungeons & Dragons* and other fantasy games. Here I quote, ". . . after years of study of the history of occultism, after having researched a book on the subject, and after having consulted with scholars in the field of historical research, I can say with confidence: these games are the most effective, most magnificently packaged, most profitably marketed, most throughly researched introduction to the occult in man's recorded history."

As the popularity of *Dungeons & Dragons* grows, so does the power of Witchcraft—one of the **Twelve Forbidden Practices** named by God:

Twelve Forbidden Practices

1. **Enchantments**
   The act of influencing by charms and incantations
   the practice of magical arts.

   > Exodus 7:11, 22; 8:7
   > Leviticus 19:26
   > Deuteronomy 18:10
   > Numbers 23:23; 24:1
   > II Kings 17:17; 21:6
   > II Chronicles 33:6
   > Ecclesiates 10:11
   > Isaiah 47:9, 12
   > Jeremiah 27:9

   Exodus 7:11, 22—*Then Pharoah also called the wise men and the sorcerers: now the magicians of Egypt, they also did in like manner with their enchantments. And the magicians of Egypt did so with their enchantments: and Pharoah's heart was hardened, neither did he hearken unto them; as the Lord hath said.*

   Exodus 8:7—*And the magicians did so with their enchantments, and brought up frogs upon the land of Egypt.*

   Leviticus 19:26—*Ye shall not eat anything with the blood: neither shall ye use enchantment, nor observe times.*

   II Chronicles 33:6—*And he caused his children to pass through the fire in the valley of the son of Hinnom: also he observed times, and used enchantments, and used witchcraft, and dealt with a familiar spirit, and with wizards: he wrought much evil in the sight of the Lord, to provoke him to anger.*

25

Jeremiah 27:9—*Therefore hearken not ye to your prophets, nor to your diviners, nor to your dreamers, nor to your enchanters, nor to your sorcerers, which speak unto you, saying, Ye shall not serve the king of Babylon.*

Enchanter

Sorcerer, magician, one who uses the human voice or music to bring another person under psychic control.

> Leviticus 19:26
> Deuteronomy 18:10-12
> II Kings 17:17
> II Chronicles 33:6
> Isaiah 47:8-11
> Jeremiah 27:9
> Daniel 1:20

Deuteronomy 18:10-12—*There shall not be found among you any one that maketh his son or his daughter to pass through the fire, or that useth divination, or an observer of times, or an enchanter, or a witch, or a charmer, or a consulter with familiar spirits, or a wizard, or a necromancer. For all that do these things are an abomination unto the Lord: and because of these abominations the Lord thy God doth drive them out from before thee.*

Daniel 1:20—*And in all matters of wisdom and understanding, that the king inquired of them, he found them ten times better than all the magicians and astrologers that were in all his realm.*

II Kings 17:17—*And they caused their sons and their daughters to pass through the fire, and used divination and enchantments, and sold themselves to do evil in the sight of the Lord, to provoke him to anger.*

27

2. **Witchcraft**

The practice of dealing with evil spirits, the use of sorcery or magic.

> Exodus 22:18
> Deuteronomy 18:10-12
> I Samuel 15:23
> II Kings 9:22
> II Chronicles 33:6
> Micah 5:12
> Nahum 3:4
> Galatians 5:19-21

Exodus 22:18—*Thou shalt not suffer a witch to live.*

I Samuel 15:23—*For rebellion is as the sin of witchcraft, and stubborness is as iniquity and idolatry. Because thou hast rejected the word of the Lord, he hath also rejected thee from being king.*

Micah 5:12—*And I will cut off witchcrafts out of thine hand; and thou shalt have no more soothsayers:*

Galatians 5:19-21—*Now the works of the flesh are manifest, which are these; Adultery, fornication, uncleanness, lasciviousness, idolatry, witchcraft, hatred, variance, emulations, wrath, strife, seditions, heresies, envyings, murders, drunkeness, revellings, and such like: of the which I tell you before, as I have also told you in time past, that they which do such things shall not inherit the kingdom of God.*

3. **Sorcery (Pharmaika)**

The use of power gained from the assistance or control of evil spirits, especially for divining.

> Exodus 7:11
> Isaiah 47:9, 12, 57:3
> Jeremiah 27:9
> Daniel 2:2
> Malachi 3:5
> Revelation 9:21; 18:23; 21:8; 22:15

Malachi 3:5—*And I will come near to you to judgement; and I will be a swift witness against the sorcerers, and against the adulterers, and against false swearers, and against those that oppress the hireling in his wages, the widow, and the fatherless, and that turn aside the stranger from his right, and fear not me, saith the Lord of hosts.*

Revelation 21:8:—*But the fearful, and unbelieving, and the abominable, and murderers, and whoremongers, and sorcerers, and idolaters, and all liars, shall have their part in the lake which burneth with fire and brimstone: which is the second death.*

4. **Divination**

Fortune-telling.

> Numbers 22:7
> II Kings 18:10-14
> Jeremiah 27:8-9
> Jeremiah 29:8-9
> Acts 16: 16-24

Jeremiah 29:8-9—*For thus saith the Lord of hosts, the God of Israel; Let not your prophets and your diviners, that be in the midst of you, deceive you, neither hearken to your dreams which ye caused to be dreamed. For they prophesy unto you in my name: I have not sent them, saith the Lord.*

5. **Wizardry**
   The art or practices of a wizard; sorcery.
   Wizard
   One skilled in magic; sorcerer; male witch (to destroy in Israel).

   > Exodus 22:18
   > Leviticus 19:31; 20:6, 27
   > Deuteronomy 18:11
   > II Kings 17:17
   > II Kings 21:6, 23:24
   > II Chronicles 33:6
   > Isaiah 8:19; 19:3

   Leviticus 19:31—*Regard not them that have familiar spirits, neither seek after wizards, to be defiled by them: I am the Lord your God.*

   Leviticus 20:27—*A man also or a woman that hath a familiar spirit, or that is a wizard, shall surely be put to death: they shall stone them with stones: their blood shall be upon them.*

   II Kings 23:24—*Moreover the workers with familiar spirits, and the wizards, and the images, and the idols, and all the abominations that were spied in the land of Judah and in Jerusalem, did Josiah put away, that he might perform the words of the law which were written in the book that Hilkiah the priest found in the house of the Lord.*

6. **Necromancy**
   Communication with the dead; conjuration of the spirits of the dead for purposes of magically revealing the future or influencing the course of events.

   > Deuteronomy 18:11
   > I Samuel 28:1-25
   > I Chronicles 10:13-14
   > Isaiah 8:19

   Isaiah 8:19—*And when they shall say unto you, Seek unto them that have familiar spirits, and unto wizards that peep, and that mutter: should not a people seek unto their God? for the living to the dead?*

7. **Charm**

Put a spell upon someone; to affect by magic.

Deuteronomy 18:11
Isaiah 19:3

Isaiah 19:3—*And the spirit of Egypt shall fail in the midst thereof; and I will destroy the counsel thereof: and they shall seek to the idols, and to the charmers, and to them that have familiar spirits, and to the wizards.*

8. **Star Gazing / Astrology**
   The divination or the supposed influence of the stars upon human affairs and terrestrial events by their positions and aspects.

   > Isaiah 47:12-15
   > Jeremiah 10:2
   > Daniel 1:18-20
   > Daniel 2:1 49
   > Daniel 4:1-37
   > Daniel 5:7-15

   Jeremiah 10:2—*Thus saith the Lord, Learn not the way of the heathen, and be not dismayed at the signs of heaven; for the heathen are dismayed at them.*

9. **Soothsaying**

The act of foretelling events; prophesying by a spirit other than the Holy Spirit.

> Joshua 13:22
> Micah 5:12-15
> Acts 16:16-18

Micah 5:12-15—*And I will cut off witchcrafts out* of thine hand; and thou shalt have no more soothsayers: Thy graven images also will I cut off, and thy standing images out of the midst of thee; and thou shalt no more worship the work of thine hands. And I will pluck up thy groves out of the midst of thee; so will I destroy thy cities. And I will execute vengeance in anger and fury upon the heathen, such as they have not heard.

10. **Prognostication**

To foretell from signs or symptoms; prophesying without the Holy Spirit; soothsaying.

> Isaiah 47:12-15
> Joshua 13:22
> Micah 5:12-15
> Acts 16:16-18

Isaiah 47:12-15—*Stand now with thine enchantments, and with the multitude of thy sorceries, wherein thou hast laboured from thy youth; if so be thou shalt be able to profit, if so be thou mayest prevail. Thou art wearied in the multitude of thy counsels. Let now the astrologers, the stargazers, the monthly prognosticators, stand up, and save thee from these things that shall come upon thee. Behold, they shall be as stubble; the fire shall burn them; they shall not deliver themselves from the power of the flame: there shall not be a coal to warm at, nor fire to sit before it. Thus shall they be unto thee with whom thou has laboured, even thy merchants, from thy youth: they shall wander every one to his quarter; none shall save thee.*

11. **Observing Times**
    Astrology.

> Leviticus 19:26
> Deuteronomy 18:10-14
> II Kings 21:6
> II Chronicles 33:6

II Kings 21:6—*And he made his son pass through the fire, and observed times, and used enchantments, and dealt with familiar spirits and wizards: he wrought much wickedness in the sight of the Lord, to provoke him to anger.*

12. **Magic**
    Witchcraft.

    > Deuteronomy 18:10-12
    > II Chronicles 33:6
    > I Samuel 15:23

    Deuteronomy 18:10-12—*There shall not be found among you any one that maketh his son or his daughter to pass through fire, or that useth divination, or an observer of times, or an enchanter, or a witch, or a charmer, or a consulter with familiar spirits, or a wizard, or a necromancer. For all that do these things are an abomination unto the Lord: and because of these abominations the Lord thy God doth drive them out from before thee.*[6]

5

The Game Of
Dungeons & Dragons

- The magician sets off a "charm person" spell.
- Thieves ransack a house.
- Characters destroy another by setting its roof on fire.

The players of this particular game of *Dungeons and Dragons* are medical school students in their 20's and the DM, a professor at the University of Southern California School of Medicine and a physician. One kindly physician's favorite character is a sub-moronic dwarf who constantly chants "Kill! Kill!" Hack, slash, loot, pillage, and burn prevail in the game. The "Level of violence runs high. There is hardly a game in which players do not indulge in murder, arson, torture, rape, or highway robbery,"[7] states the game's

Dungeon Master. The dwarf character drinks too much, tries to sexually assault a female character, gets into a fight and lands in the castle dungeon.

Enthusiasts of *D & D* say that the Dungeon Master must provide an interesting game. The characters should always feel a sense of danger and lurking menace but should be able to swagger through much of their world with the firm knowledge that they are heroes. Unfortunately for some, the make-believe world assumes an eerie sense of reality.

"This is really the first commercial attempt to provide a game where the players can really use their imaginations and ingenuity freely," says Gary Gyax himself. "If you run into a dragon sitting on a pile of treasure, you can attack it and attempt to slay it. You can try to negotiate with it. You can use trickery. You can run away if you don't think you can handle it, and maybe come back another time..." or you can get unlucky and be burned to a crisp by its breath.[8]

Let's Look At The Player Characters:

In *D & D* there are seven races from which a player can choose:

1. dwarf
2. elf
   (the above can see in the dark)

3. gnome
4. half-elf
5. halfling
6. half-orc
7. human

Occupations from which a player can choose:

Cleric	Wears armor and carries weapons but may not draw blood; therefore restricted to blunt weapons; can do spells and heal wounds.
Druid	Cleric of nature with powers over animals and plants.
Fighter	Wears all types of armor that he can afford; wields any weapon.
Paladin	Fighter of holy order sworn to chastity and goodness, like the Knights of the Round Table.
Ranger	Lone woodsman with special tracking and possibly magical abilities.
Magic User	Mighty spells are limited; he can only use a small number of spells per game; carries only a dagger.
Illusionist	Magic user whose spells are limited to those which deceive the senses.
Thief	Wears light armor; detects trap doors, secret panels; picks locks and pockets; hides in shadows and climbs sheer walls.

Assassin	Thief/monk who specializes in lethal attack.
Monk	Specialist in "kung fu" type of barehanded combat and other abilities.
Bard	Casts magic spells by singing; fighter.[9]

Characters develop as adventures unfold. Accumulated treasures allow a character to hire a handful of assassins, slaves, etc. Characters become harder to kill because of increased "hit points." In *D & D* a character can receive a certain number of injuries or "hits" without consequence. As a character lives through game after game, he becomes more indestructible, able to receive attacks by more and more severe weapons without being weakened. Their increased level of experience allows them to become more and more powerful in battle.

D & D offers the player the opportunity to cast himself into roles associated with demon powers. In his imagination he assumes the role of a sorcerer or some super-human character who possesses extra-ordinary abilities. It is through the casting of spells and enchantments that he breaks the powers of others seeking to destroy him on his quest for treasure.

Magic/Gods

". . . every player at some point, particularly if he's a Wizard, decides he's going to start manufacturing his own potions and making his own magic items," Gygax is quoted as saying.[10]

In *D & D* the characters are magical or super powerful; They venture into a dangerous situation in search of treasure and are attacked by magical mythological creatures. With a little skill and luck they defeat the monsters and carry off a treasure of gold, magic, or other valuables.

The rules allow for resurrection and reincarnation, and characters have superhuman or magical powers. A Dungeon Master can offer as alternatives to death wish rings or resurrection. A cleric can heal by the laying on of hands.

Dungeons and Dragons promotes the pagan concept of more than one god, divine intervention, and healing. When placed into an impossible situation one character responded to the DM's question "What are you going to do?" with, "I'm going to get down on my knees and pray real hard." The DM Guide allows for Divine Intervention with a basic roll for success of 100. Odds are softened if one is a cleric of the deity evoked, has been particularly devout, or is in a situation the Divine Will would be sure to disapprove.

"Hit Points" can be restored, if the blow is not fatal, by clerical healing spells, potions and rest. Gods of Good are noted as being Solinari and Habbakuk. Hiddukel and Zeboim are Gods of Evil.

Dial *D* & *D*

Those who are obsessed with *D* & *D* can now add a new dimension to their "Fantasy Gaming." Just pick up your touch-tone telephone, dial a certain number, and you can "experience a Dungeon adventure which you control. You make decisions which direct your adventure by dialing numbers..."

"The creatures and deadly traps which await you are brought to life with dramatic sound effects. Hear the Roar of the Flesh eater as you lock swords, The Sizzle of the fireball bursting towards you, The Clinking of the Gold Pieces you will find in The Demon Prince's underground Dungeon."[11]

6
Who Plays
Dungeons & Dragons?

"It is just because bloodshed, mayhem and murder are impossible, but not unthinkable to the majority of us civilized folks, that a fantasy in which we get to act out such forbidden temptations is so attractive," says John Eric Holmes who is an avid *D & D* player as well as an author and medical school professor. "I think fantasy of some sort is the normal human way to deal with frustration and uncertainty. It is the charm and nostalgia of an adult game of 'Let's pretend' that draw most of us to the game. We really want to believe the fantasy characters are real, in some universe parallel to our own...we talk about our imaginary selves as if they did have a separate existence—a separate existence much more glamorous and exciting than our own. Role playing, like other forms of fantasy on film, tape, or papers is an escape. Some people seem to need this type of escape. The fact that most game players are young males suggests that these people have a special need for escape fantasy. It fulfills the secret desire we all cherish, to find a world where the heroes are always handsome, the heroines always lovely, good is always beautiful and evil is always ugly. It is a world as one would like it to be, peopled by a finer, or at least more powerful, version of our very selves."[12]

The role playing game makes a fantasy epic. The player becomes the hero. He must make the decisions, perform the actions, and take the risks that a fictional hero might. In a good game, the sense of personal involvement is immediate. The players say things like:

- "I jump to the top of the rock,"
- "I draw my sword,"
- "I prepare my most powerful spell."

A player carefully guides his character through hour after hour of adventures. Since the rules of the game of *Dungeons and Dragons* allow only one character per player at a time, he equates with his character almost to the alter-ego state. Therefore, when a character gets killed, the player is apt to go into a depression—usually brief, but quite real. The characters of a fantasy game take on a life of their own. The players begin to think of them as having an independent existence, somewhere in another dimension of space and time. No one who does not play *D & D* can understand the shock that comes with the violent death of one's character. It is a little piece of the player that gets killed. For the very young player, this death may be a bit too much. The thoughtful Dungeon Master provides for this as the rules allow resurrection and reincarnation.

"Consumers tend to be males who are bright, analytical and tireless," says Michael S. Dobson, Director of Marketing, TSR Inc.[13] The typical role-playing gamer is a teenaged white male from a middle class background. He is above average in intelligence and interested in math and science. He is not particularly athletic and he reads a lot, especially science fiction and fantasy. He has a small circle of friends, mostly his own age, with whom he plays the game on a weekly or even daily basis. An unusually high percentage of these teenaged gamers will go on to college. The other attribute they all possess, of course, is an extremely active imagination.[14]

Dungeon Masters play the game differently. Some dislike situations in which characters get killed. Others feel a game is successful only when half the players die in battle. DM's sometimes begin to think "I wonder what *really* is beyond the Southern jungle," forgetting that he alone has the *power* to put something there. The make-believe world assumes an eerie sense of reality.

"The 'alternate universe' feel to the world of *Dungeons and Dragons* is produced by its *social* reality. It is a shared fantasy, not a solitary one, and the group spirit contributes to the tremendous appeal of the game," states *Psychology Today*. "The Dungeon Master's world is sort of a giant Rorschack Test."[15]

7

A "Fun" Game?

Although Gary Gygax contends the game is harmless and just a "fun" game, he does admit that the game can cause players to become too personally involved. "When you start playing out a fantasy, it can really eat up time and capture you totally," he told a reporter. "Most people can handle it, but there probably are exceptions. You can get very emotionally involved. I've got several characters I've nurtured through many tension-filled, terror-fraught D & D games, and I'd be really crushed if I lost one of them. They can become very much a part of you."[16]

The Society for Creative Anachronism is one example of a group of people who have become too involved in the game, to the point of obsession.[17] This nationwide, underground war-gaming club is comprised of members who wear medieval clothing—swords, steel helmets and all—and who adopt the lifestyle of their characters, even going so far as to wage live wars on fellow society members.

The war-gaming club is not alone in the examples of people who have become obsessed with fantasy role-playing games. Gygax himself says the makeup of D & D leads itself to an undisciplined overindulgence. "You have to pursue D & D with you whole soul if you're going do do well at it."[18] And when "pursuing the game with his whole soul," a player often has difficulty differentiating between the game and reality. This can be seen as one young man, who is an avid D & D player, recalls his ordeal to a reporter.[19] The young man was a sophomore, majoring in chemistry, at Michigan State University.

> He had been alone inside a musty fortress, lost in a maze of dank passageways that hid mortal dangers. He was armed only with a sword and a shield, scant protection from the grotesque monster that lurked there, waiting for him.
>
> Unable to escape, he had faced the creature, a huge, hairy, fire-breathing nightmare for which the young man had been no match in battle.
>
> "It killed me," he said. "Burned me to death."
>
> The young man's mood was serious. He said his hands were perspiring as he recounted the confrontation. He knew he was not dead. He knew he was not dead. He knew that the fortress and the monster had not been real. But the memory of the fantasy he and several friends had created the night before was very real and it had shaken him badly.
>
> And he said he loved it.

"Fantasies, in and of themselves, serve a healthy function, like relieving boredom," says Michigan psychologist Dr. Jack McGaugh.[20] "Like any good thing, it can be overdone. What you think about, you become at the time."

The game's creator, Gary Gygax, admits that D & D players are fervid followers. "They ARE dedicated. They get really caught up in it. But I've met some obsessed golfers and tennis players, too. *Dungeons and Dragons* is just a different kind of release."[21]

When Gygax and Dave Arneson, of Lake Geneva, Wisconsin, created the game, its biggest suporters were college students. For them, *D & D* offered an escape from the intense demands of college academia.[22] As the game increased in popularity, post-college adults started playing. And eventually, the interest filtered down to the pre-teen age groups. Today, many secondary schools even offer "talented and gifted" students the opportunity to play *D & D* for credit during school hours. Some "classroom versions" of the game are even being produced. Many state-supported colleges are offering classes in *D & D*; however, there are also many who have cancelled them at the insistence of concerned parents and taxpayers. Still, college students are the game's strongest following.

"It (the game) allows you to work out frustrations and the doldrums of classes," one coed from Oakland University in Pontiac, Michigan, told a reporter. "You get away from everything. You can do anything you want to do, anything your wildest imagination will permit. But it's not dangerous. Sometimes I'm too busy creating dungeons and rolling up characters to do my homework, but I don't go out and live out my fantasies. Only nuts go into steam tunnels."[23]

According to Dieter H. Sturm, spokesman for the firm that markets *Dungeons and Dragons*, in 1983 there were three or four million *D & D* players in the United States.[24] There is also a strong *D & D* following in England and France.[25] According to the *Model Retailer* magazine, in 1980, *D & D* was equal in terms of national popularity with any board game, including *Monoply*.[26] However, fantasy role-playing games still ranked behind electronic games in popularity.[27] Despite the fact that *Dungeons and Dragons* is equal in terms of popularity to any board game,

D & D adherents do no play the game like any other. There are some who just "dabble," but there are also "real-lifers" who have basically lost all interest and motivation in the real world. These people spend all their waking hours in search of treasures at the expense of orcs and dragons. But the majority of players fall somewhere in between the two extremes, meeting once or twice a week, with a normal game lasting four to six hours.[28]

8

Zealots

Players love the character's growth and change, the alliance and back-stabbing, the quest . . . players are wizards for the duration of the game. Most are content to play the game on paper in their homes, but some of the aficionadoes have been known to dress up in medieval costumes and get physically involved in the action.

Some *D & D* zealots carry the game to extremes. At the University of North Carolina, students complain that players overload the school's computer with complex scenarios. In Austin, Texas, fans meet each Sunday for *D & D* combat practice, dressed in medieval attire and armed with rattan replicas of ancient weaponry. "I've seen some people become so involved that they try to become their characters," observes Scott Jacobs, a political science student at the University of Georgia. "But most players understand that it is just a game."[29] True, some *D & D* players realize that this phenomenon is simply a game, but far too many enthusiasts harm others either intentionally or inadvertently in their pursuit of the "perfect game of *D & D*." Let's take a look at some of the players.

Player Profile: Gary Huckabay

"It's fun to put half-orc babies in a catapult and fire them at a wall. They splat very nicely. I also enjoy cutting off their eyelashes, mopping their faces with a mace and melting them with green slime," says Gary Huckabay, an avid *D & D* player. "When I compare my real life and the life I lead as a Dungeon Master, there is no doubt in my mind as to which is the richer."

He defends the game by saying, "I've never met a player who thought a game was really happening. It is just a creative way of relieving your frustrations on a symbolic level. Some people scrunch their wives. I scrunch monsters instead."

Gary started reading when he was two, started making up new games at 4, and at 8 was designing new buildings. At 10 he started dreaming up new life forms. At 12 he discovered a world that combined everything he loved — stories, games, architecture and the creation of a new species—the world of *Dungeons and Dragons.*

Gary is a scholar of fantasy. Leading fugures of Greek mythology and medieval history are as familiar to him as the characters in TV serials are to most boys his age. When not actually playing, Gary spends his evenings on dungeon diagrams, character records and descriptions of new monsters, deities, and spells which have filled 1500 pages. In class he daydreams about the traps and tortures that will await his friends as soon as he can shuck the humdrum guise of a high school student and in a blinding metamorphosis become a wizard, a god.

Gary has spent a year designing and mapping his dungeon. It has eleven levels—ten of which are covered with algae, filth, and slime. They even have carrion and dead bodies floating around. This, to him, is the life that is richer.

Gary has chosen the evil alignment for his characters. Gary explains "If I don't like a law, I break it. If I don't like a player, I kill him. Evil characters have so much more freedom, don't you think?"

He estimates he has spent over $2000 on *D & D*, mostly for transportation to conventions, and over 6000 hours developing a private *D & D* computer simulation on his Apple II home computer. All of his close friends are also *D & D* players. [30]

Player Profile: James Dallas Egbert III

Dungeon Master: The Disappearance Of James Dallas Egbert III is a book authored by William Dear. Mr. Dear was hired by Dallas Egbert's parents to find their son, a 16-year-old sophomore at Michigan State. Dallas vanished from that campus in the summer of 1979 under suspicious circumstances. Dallas was an avid *D & D* player, and Michigan State had a real dungeon—8½ miles of tunnels of steam pipes, a black, hot maze, which networked under the campus. These were full of false leads, blind corners, and hidden rooms and the real danger of being injured by hot steam jets. Against the rules of the school, students often acted out their *D & D* games within the tunnels. Dallas was one of these students, and it was following such a game that he was found missing. A lot of controversy arose from the incident. The tunnels were blocked off and *D & D* was banned from the campus.

Dallas was a genius who could not make himself understood and had an obsessive need for detail and control. Dear did finally find the runaway Dallas, who wrote after he reappeared, "I'll give Satan my mind and power." Dallas had suffered a marked personality change during his heavy involvement with *Dungeons and Dragons*. The depression characterized by his *D & D* obsession led him one year later to kill himself. This was cited as proof of the game's harmfulness.[31]

9

A "Deadly" Game

The National Coalition on Television Violence has linked heavy involvement with the violence-oriented fantasy role-playing war games to over 90 deaths. These include 62 murders, 26 suicides, and two deaths of undetermined causes. According to evidence from police reports, courtroom trials, and family interviews, *Dungeons & Dragons* is said to have played a decisive role in causing 37 of the 90 deaths. In the other cases, a heavy involvement into *D & D* is considered to have been a major factor leading to the suicides or murders involved.

Recent deaths include the case of a 16 year-old New York boy, David K. Ventriquattro, who was convicted of killing an 11 year-old fellow *D & D* player following a game. He told police that the younger boy had become "evil" in the fantasy and it was his role to "extinguish the evil."[32]

Two soldiers, dressed in ninja martial arts outfits slit the throats of an elderly couple while stealing their jewelry during a break-in. A *D & D* martial arts book was found on the dashboard of the truck used by the soldiers.

A 17 year-old Canaan, New York honor student, Wyley Gates fatally shot four people as part of an elaborate game of *D & D* Wyley murdered his father, brother, cousin, and his father's girlfriend after he had been playing a game that he had code-named "Infierno," a reference to Dante's *Inferno*. It was also discovered that Wyley and two other students had reportedly stolen parts of two computers and disks from their high school to enable them to keep track of their complicated game.[33] Another adolescent boy shot his brother to death and tried to kill two family members while engaged in *D & D* fantasies.

Other gamesmen have left suicide notes and diaries linking *D & D* as a cause of their deaths. Pat Pulling, mother of a boy who killed himself, founded an organization called Bothered About Dungeons and Dragons (B.A.D.D.). Pulling said that her son played *D & D* at the time of his suicide. He had become so wrapped up in the game that his grades had begun to suffer, and when another player in a long-running game in the Gifted and Talented Program at his school sent him a curse of suicidal mania, he interpreted it literally—and shot himself in the heart. A suicide note clearly linked the game with his death. Pulling described the game manuals as containing "detailed descriptions of killing, satanic human sacrifice, assassination, sadism, premeditated murder, and curses of insanity." She added that much of the material comes from "demonology, including witchcraft, the occult and evil monsters."

Timothy Grice, 21, committed suicide by shooting himself with a shotgun. He was a *D & D* fanatic and Dungeon Master with half of his bedroom covered by *D & D* material. Two self-written manuscripts were found open near his body. The detective report states that apparently *D & D* became a reality to this young college honors student when he thought that he could leave his body and return. Grice was following directions on "astral travel" from the manual at the time of his death. He thought that since he was not "inside" his body, the bullet would not injure him. A similar death was reported in California. Juan Kimbrough, 14, asked his brother to shoot him, stating that he was a Dungeon Master with special powers and could not be hurt.

Thomas E. Radecki, M.D., NCTV Research Director and psychiatrist, has participated in five of the *Dungeons and Dragons* burglary and murder trials and has had minor cases in his own psychiatry practice. In a press interview he said, "From official investigations, from the adolescent murders and criminal defendants that I have examined, and from my own practice, I have no doubt that these games are causing dozens of deaths, as well as a much larger number of more minor problems. The evidence is overwhelming. Any honest epidemiologic study of these cases would have to conclude that these violent role-playing games are having a serious harmful effect on many young people. While perhaps a hundred young people have been led to murder and suicide, the evidence suggests that thousands have committed more minor anti-social behavior and hundreds of thousands have become desensitized to violence."

NCTV says that in over 80 cases, *Dungeons and Dragons* has been involved because of its numerous mentions of human sacrifice and the drinking of blood, because characters can be brought back from the dead repeatedly, and because players sometimes choose demonic gods to worship as part of the game. Twenty-two different types of satanic demons and evils can be part of the game and there are dozens of spells of occult magic with some of the material lifted straight out of demonology. NCTV also reports that this led to an involvement in Satan worship in ten of the murders and suicides.

The game entails various attacks, assasinations, spying, theft, and poisonings. Players can arm their characters with any of 62 different types of weapons. There are 39 different tools that players can use in their torture chambers, 11 types of mercenary soldiers that players can hire who have tendencies to pillage and rape, and 11 types of prostitutes possible in the game. There are tables for racial hatred and players are encouraged to consult these when hiring mercenaries for their armies.

Combat armor, medieval weaponry, spells and curses, and many forms of mental attack are involved. Holy/unholy water, magic of all types, ESP, mental telepathy, and military combat fill the game. Players can be cursed with 20 different types of insanity.

Dr. Radecki gave two cases from his own psychiatric practice. One involved a 12 year-old boy who underwent a personality change after getting too involved with the Dungeons & Dragons game. He became too aggressive for his single mother to handle and had to be placed in foster care. In the second case, Radecki hospitalized a 26 year-old woman because of mental exhaustion due to an intense harassment by a former roommate. The roommate had gotten into *D & D* and then into Satan worship with her *D & D* friends. She was making repeated harassing telephone calls, painted a pentagram on the patient's home and made several attempts to kidnap the patient's 9 year-old daughter. According to Radecki, the *D & D* group had apparently gotten into animal sacrifice at a city park only blocks from his hospital.

NCTV and B.A.D.D. said that in at least 37 instances where young men have murdered themselves or others, there is "very solid evidence—including police reports, eyewitnesses and documents left by the victims—that *D & D's* influence was a decisive factor.[34]

Fifty-three other cases exist where *D & D* appears to have played a major role in the thinking of the young males at the time of their violence. Several non-fatal murder attempts by *D & D* groups and one rape where *D & D* played a major role have been reported. Six cases of insanity afflicting young males have been reported where *Dungeons and Dragons* appears to have played a major causal role.

10

Is Dungeons & Dragons A Religion?

Although *D & D* is not a religion per se, it does teach religious principles and familiarize players with terms and rituals of occult forms of religion. A few years ago, the game came under fire when many groups claimed the game was "anti-religious, filled with pictures and symbols you could find in any basic witchcraft book." But Gygax is quick to defend his demons: "The game is neither good nor evil. It is simply a good time, and for some students, a tool to learn." As for the witchcraft found in the book: "I made up all the spells out of my head. How can anyone take them seriously? The ingredient in one of the spells is 'legumes.' "[35]

Despite Gygax's denial that the game is occult, there are many references to traditional Christian terms, such as atonement, deity, faith, fasting, resurrection, God, prayer and Divine Ascension, that are treated in a blasphemous manner in the players' handbooks and various other *D & D* guide books.

According to the *American College Encyclopedia Dictionary*, blasphemy is the "impious utterance or action concerning God or sacred things; the crime of assuming to oneself the rights or qualities of God; and the irreverant behavior toward anything held sacred."

Some examples of blasphemy are found in quotes taken from the more than 20 books that teach how to play *Dungeons and Dragons*:

Concerning "Deities" and "Gods"

"This game lets all your fantasies come true. This is a world where monsters, dragons, good and evil, high priests, fierce demons, and even the gods themselves may enter your character's life."[36]

In other sections the gods are referred to as 'deity':

(1) "It is well known by all experienced players . . . spells bestowed upon them by their respective deities.[37]

(2) "Each cleric must have his or her own deity."[38]

(3) "The deity (you the DM 'Dungeon Master') will point out all the transgressions . . . ."[39]

"Serving a deity is a significant part of *D & D*, and all player characters should have a patron god. Alignment assumes its full importance when tied to the worship of a deity."[40]

"Changing alignment: Whether or not the character actively professes some deity, he or she will have an alignment and serve one or more deities of this general alignment indirectly or unbeknownst to the character."[41]

Concerning Prayer and Fasting

"Clerical spells . . . are bestowed by the gods, so that the cleric need but pray for a few hours . . . ."[42]

"If the Cleric desires third through fifth level spells, the monions (angels, demigods, or whatever) will be likely to require the cleric to spend two to eight days in prayer, fasting, and contemplation of his or her transgression, making whatever sacrifices and atonement are necessary . . . Spell recovery . . . requires about the same period of time in order to pray and meditate . . . ."[43]

Concerning Magic and Spells

"Swords and sorcery best describe what this game is all about . . . so mind unleashing, that it comes near reality."[44]

"Most spells have a verbal component and so must be uttered."[45]

"The spell caster should be required to show you what form of protective inscription he or she has used when the spell is cast. According to experts in witchcraft and Satanic worship the three forms mentioned are: Pictures of a magic circle, pentagram, and thaumaturgic triangle."[46]

Concerning Clerics

"Another important attribute of the cleric is the ability to turn away (or actually command into service) the undead and less powerful demons and devils."[47]

Concerning Death

"Resurrection" is referred to as "the revival of a character after its death by magical means."[48]

Concerning Satanism

"Elric (hero)"—the sign being given by his left hand (which is called the Goat Head sign) means "Satan is lord" to all Satan worshippers.[49]

The word "demon" appears 106 times in pages 16-19 of the Monster Manual. And the player has been told to trust four of these demons as (lesser gods) on page 105, paragraph 5, of the Deities and Demigods book.

The word "devil" appears 94 times and the word "hell" appears 25 times in pages 20-23 of the Monster Manual.

Concerning Defilement

In the following excerpt from page 115 of the Players Handbook, blesses and curses, and unholy and holy are treated as equals.

"Defilement of Fonts: If any non-believer blesses/curses an unholy/holy font, or uses less refined means such as excreting wastes into a font or basin, the whole is absolutely desecrated, defiled, and unfit . . . Note that either method of defilement requires actual contact with the font and its vessel. Any blessing or cursing from a distance will be absolutely ineffectual and wasted."

Consider the following story about John, a 16-year-old sophomore at a Southern California college.

He sits in his small dorm room, $900 worth of handpainted miniatures covering the bed.

"Ever since I was 10, I've wanted to drop out of this world. There are so many flaws. A lot of things are unfair. When I'm in my own world, I control my own world order. I can picture it all. The groves and trees. The beauty. I can hear the wind. The world isn't like that. My beliefs, morals, sense of right and wrong are much stronger since playing *D & D*," he says.

But, in comparison, the real world becomes less tenable.

"It's hazardous. Your vocabulary, your mental quickness increases, but school seems increasingly boring and droll. Your grades drop. The more time you spend in your fantasy world, the more you want to walk away from the burdensome decisions of life.

"The more I play *D & D*, the more I want to get away from this world. The whole thing is getting very bad."[50]

We must recognize the dangers of our children spending so much time playing this game. It often leads to a distortion of reality, as well as filling the child's mind with images of the occult.

11

What's Wrong With Dungeons & Dragons?

Some people claim that games such as *Dungeons and Dragons* are harmless, strictly for fun, fantasy, and entertainment. Beware! They are not! Parents who allow such games are playing with dynamite—and, their children's souls. They open their homes, and their children's minds to subtle introduction to the occult and the malignant world of psychotherapy (mind alteration and values modification). There is nothing benign about these games. They are part of the increasing spread of the occult, a push that will increase in tempo and furor as Satan's time grows shorter.

Dungeons and Dragons is not a game. Instead, some believe it to be a teaching the following:

- demonology
- witchcraft
- voodoo
- murder
- rape

- blasphemy
- suicide
- assassination
- insanity
- sex perversion
- homosexuality
- prostitution
- Satan worship
- gambling
- Jungian psychology
- barbarism
- cannibalism
- sadism
- desecration
- demon summoning
- necromantics
- divination

When thou art come into the land which the Lord thy God giveth thee, thou shalt not learn to do after the abominations of those nations. There shall not be found among you any one that maketh his son or his daughter to pass through the fire, or that uses divination, or an observer of times, or an enchanter, or a witch. Or a charmer, or a consulter with familiar spirits, or a wizard or a necro-mancer. For all that do these things are an abomination of the Lord . . . (Deuteronomy 18:9-12).

Students who participate in *Dungeons and Dragons* are laid open to a subtle, but very powerful form of spiritual, mental, moral, and thus behavioral conditioning that is extremely dangerous for several reasons.

The first is violence. Persons participating in *D & D* find themselves in a lifestyle where killing, robbery, maiming, destruction, sexual abuse, fear, confusion, hatred and rebellion are the norm. Players experience values modification. In the universe of *D & D*, good is no better or more powerful than evil. In other words, good and evil are presented as equal and opposite poles. Players align themselves with one or the other. However, those who choose good are inhibited while those who adopt evil character traits are more free to pursue selfish goals. There are no penalties for evil conduct.

When young people become intensely and emotionally involved with role-playing with this type of base, traditional moral values are destroyed. Personal advancement becomes the guiding factor, and ethics are tossed out the window. The more deeply a person becomes enmeshed in such role-playing, the more his old value system comes under attack. Undesireable real life behavior becomes more likely.

Dungeons and Dragons encourages reality distortion. Unlike other games, *D & D* presents an alternative universe loaded with spine-chilling excitement. Players mentally enter into the plot, everything is happening around them. They must make life-or-death decisions. Since this is a shared fantasy, the more players that share the fantasy, the more blurred becomes the line between that and reality. Persons who feel inadequate, bored, or alienated from society can be brought to a position where *D & D's* alternative realities are much more exciting and fulfilling than real life. The results are:

- Withdrawl from society
- Paranoia
- Suppressed or expressed hostility

Players can become so emotionally bonded to their characters that when the character is killed, the player becomes devastated to the point of depression. The game is counter productive. Children or youth who become deeply involved in *Dungeons and Dragons* often spend a vast amount of their waking time and creative energies playing, thinking, dreaming about and planning *D & D* strategies.

Dungeons and Dragons teaches an occult form of religion. Even in its most basic form, the players are introduced to magic, the casting of spells, the use of magic circles, pentagrams, and other psychic devices. Players battle or seek the aid of demons and pagan deities. They are encouraged to align themselves with and worship a deity or deities.

While *Dungeons & Dragons* players do not in reality practice demon summoning, witchcraft, divination, necromantics, or Satan worship, they are opened to these possibilities. Will the young person who has found *Dungeons and Dragons* so exciting be appalled when he discovers that astral projection, divining the future, healings and the casting of spells all involve a spiritual power for him to tap?

Finally, the more a player participates in the game, the more he chooses to remain in the fantasy world, and the harder it will be for him to accept his responsibilities in the real world. We must realize the dangers of our children playing this game. It leads to a distortion of reality and fills his mind with images of the occult. The game can become an almost mystical experience, consuming, addictive, and potentially dangerous.

12

Letter From A
Dungeon Master

Have you ever spoken with a Dungeon Master? If not, here are portions of a letter from a very misguided young man who is entranced by the game of *Dungeons and Dragons*.

(Dungeon Master)

"In reading your book **Turmoil In The Toybox II** concerning *Dungeons and Dragons*, I thought I will let you know my point of view.

"The game (*Dungeons and Dragons*) focuses on one thing—mythology. Please take note—the first part of the word *myth* means untrue, false.

"It is apparent that you have researched the rule books to some extent, and if you didn't notice in the *Dungeon Master's Guide* and the new second edition version, it CLEARLY states that this game is very flexible when the rules come into play. Also in the *Players Handbooks*. The spells that require some kind of components do not state what to do with the materials. True for the spell 'spider-climb' a wizard must eat a live spider, but the player doesn't eat the thing! Also, it requires some kind of hand-gestures and verbal stuff which no spells describe!

"I have been playing *D & D* (*Dungeons and Dragons*) for 10 years, I am 19 now. For probably about 9 of those years I have been a DM. **Nobody** in my game, 'sees me as a god.' **Nobody** in my game treats their so-called 'Deities' with reverence or performs some kind of ritual to it. **Nobody** who plays clerics constantly prays for their spells, they just get them—no fasting or anything. I feel that they've played their characters well enough and have earned enough experience points to have the spells. When someone playing a wizard in my game casts a spell, they simply state that they're casting it and 'boom,'—it's done. I use no magic circles, or pentagrams or junk like that. It is assured if a wizard needs protection, a force field of some sort appears around him when the appropriate spell is cast. Turning away undead is just that. (If y'see a vampire, a cleric goes 'boo'—and he's gone. Resurrection is an alias for giving dead characters another chance—so what? I have no idea what the Goat Head sign is. I don't even believe in witches!

"The words 'demon,' 'devil,' and 'hell,' appear in the Bible, do they not? They don't make it any less Holy than it is do they? Fonts and basins are not used in blessing or cursing. It's just done if someone wants to do it."

(Author's Response)

The terms 'blessing' and 'cursing' belie this Dungeon Master's arguement. Webster defines 'blessing' as **to pronounce holy**. *Blessing can be given only to that of the Lord. Philippians 4:8 tells us:* . . . **brethren, whatever is true, whatever is honorable, whatever is just, whatever** *is pure, whatever is lovely, whatever is gracious, if there is any excellence, if there is anything worthy of praise, think about these things. What you have learned and received and heard and seen in me, do; and the peace of God will be with you.* (RSV)

(Dungeon Master)

"I guess when it comes to looking at our world in comparison to the world I run in D & D, the D & D world without a doubt is better. That's just because of all the wonders of the unicorn and dragons, wizards, great noble knights—the whole concept. It's Tolkein, King Arthur, and Robin Hood rolled all into one."

(Author's Response)

The letter writer looks upon God's world as described in Genesis and named "truly good" as not as good as his fantasy world—one of sorcerers, clerics, wizards, dragons, etc. Revelation 22:15 tells us of the gates of the Kingdom of God: **Outside are the dogs and sorcerers and fornicators, and murderers and idolaters, and everyone who loves and practices falsehood.** (NIV)

(Dungeon Master)

To continue DM's letter: "My beliefs, morals, and sense of right and wrong I feel are better—also like the 16 year-old kid you mentioned, but D & D is not #1 on my list. It's only a game—but a great stress-reliever."

(Author's Response)

Here, again I disagree with you, DM. As was already mentioned, D & D has done just the opposite in the lives of numerous players. The 100 plus documented cases of suicide and murder represent only a small percentage of the mental problems caused by D & D. No, indeed, D & D is definitely not a stress-reliever.

73

(Dungeon Master)

DM writes, "The only reason why I use gods in my games is because of the mythological nature of them. As being DM, I usually play these gods when (usually if) they're needed. Even then I don't feel him constantly, even when playing D & D. I know if this game is wrong God will stop me from playing."

(Author's Response)

Dear DM, God has made us free moral agents. We are not "robots" to be stopped. He allows us to see the rights and the wrongs of the world by studying His Word. Perhaps, you should try reading the BIBLE when you are seeking true stress relief.

(Dungeon Master)

"So as you can see," DM concludes, "every person who plays D & D is not corrupted, or turned away from Christ. This game has taught me how to co-operate with people, how to get along with them, and with God's blessing it will continue to do so . . . Jesus has provided an escape for us, but when we want to get something off our mind, there's nothing like a diversion."

(Author's Response)

Sorry, Dungeon Master, God will never bless D & D or its works. You are right when you say, "Jesus has provided an escape for us." But that escape is through Himself— not through Dungeons and Dragons.

Bibliography

1. Elshof Phyllis Ten, "D&D: A Fantasy Fad or Dabbling in the Demonic?" *Christianity Today*, September 4, 1981, p. 56.

2. "Welcome to TSR's Worlds of Opportunity For 1989 . . . ," *Toy & Hobby World*, February 1989, pp. 221-224.

3. Fadiman, Anne, "Portrait: Gary Huckabay; a teenage master of wizardry and enchantment," *Life*, March 1982, p. 17.

4. Smith, Geoffrey, "Dungeons and Dollars," *Forbes*, September 15, 1980, p. 138.

5. "Private Lives," *INC*, December 1984, p. 74.

6. Phillips, Phil and Joan Hake Robie, *Halloween And Satanism*, Lancaster, Pennsylvaina: Starburst Publishers, 1987, pp. 91-98.

7. Holmes, John Eric, "Confessions Of A Dungeon Master," *Psychology Today*, November 1980, p. 87.

8. "Dungeons and Dollars," p. 138.

9. *Dungeons And Dragons Player Handbook*

10. "Dungeons And Dollars," p. 138

11. "The World Of Fandom, Vol II, No. 7, p. 48.

12. Holmes, John Eric, *Fantasy Role Playing Games*, New York: Hippocrene Books, Inc., 1981, pp. 211 & 213.

13. Unsworth, Tim, "The TSR Story: How The Games Empire Expanded," *Publishers Weekly*, February 12, 1988, p. 66.

14. Holmes, *Fantasy Role Playing Games*, p. 206.

15. Holmes, Confessions, p. 87.

16. Heller, Jean, "Joys, Dangers of Game where One's Imagination is the Limit," *San Francisco Examiner and Chronicle*, September 23, 1979.

17. Ibid.

18. *Rolling Stone*, 1980.

19. Heller, 1979.

20. Ibid.

21. Ibid.

22. Oman, Anne H. "Dungeons and Dragons: It's Not Just a Game. It's an Adventure," *The Washington Post*, February 20, 1981, p. C2.

23. Heller, 1979.

24. Crichton, Doug, "Pair Blames Son's Suicide on Dungeons and Dragons," *Richmond Times-Dispatch*, August 11, 1983.

25. Associated Press, "Fantasy Games Find Fervid Fans," *Longview Morning Journal*, May 17, 1981, p. 8D.

26. *Model Retailer*, 1980.

27. "Dungeons and Dragons," *Cornerstone Magazine*, Chicago, Illinois, December 1980.

28. Ibid.

29. Weathers, Diane with Donna M. Foote, "Beware The Harpies!" *Newsweek*, Vol. 94:109, September 24, 1979, p. 109.

30. Fadiman, 1982.

31. Sutton, Roger, "A D&D Phenomenon," *School Library Journal*, November 1984, p. 82.

32. "16-Year-Old Is Convicted In Fantasy-Game Slaying Of Boy, 11," *New York Times*, November 23, 1986, p. 47.

33. "Slayings Of Four Tied To A Game Using Fantasies," *New York Times*, December 20, 1986, p. 30.

34. "Critics Link A Fantasy Game To 29 Deaths," *Chrsitianity Today*, May 17, 1985, p. 64.

35. Loohauis, Jackie, "Gurus of the Games," *The Milwaukee Journal*, November 19, 1981.

36. *D & D Handbook*, p. 7.

37. *Dungeon Masters Handbook*, p. 38.

38. Ibid.

39. Ibid, p. 39.

40. *Dieties and Demigods Instruction Manual*, p. 5.

41. *Dungeon Masters Guide*, p. 25.

42. *D & D Players Handbook*, p. 40.

43. *Dungeon Masters Handbook*, pp. 38-39.
44. *D & D Handbook*, p. 7.
45. *D & D Players Handbook*, p. 40.
46. *Dungeon Masters Guide*, p. 42.
47. *D & D Players Handbook*, p. 20.
48. *Dungeon Master*, p. 229.
49. *Dungeon Masters Guide*, p. 86.
50. *Cornerstone Magazine*, December 1980.

Books & Tapes by Starburst Publishers
(Partial listing—full list available on request)

Except For A Staff   —Randy R. Spencer
(trade paper) ISBN 0914984349 **$7.95**

The Quest For Truth (novel   —Ken Johnson
(trade paper) ISBN 0914984217 **$7.95**

Dragon Slaying For Parents   —Tom Prinz, M.S.
(trade paper) ISBN 0914984367 **$9.95**

Like A Bulging Wall—Will You Survive The 1990's Economic Crash?
—Robert Borrud
(trade paper) ISBN 0914984284 **$8.95**

TemperaMysticism—Exploding the Temperament Theory
—Shirley Ann Miller
(trade paper) ISBN 0914984306 **$8.95**

Reverse The Curse In Your Life   —Joan Hake Robie
(trade paper) ISBN 0914984241 **$7.95**

Teenage Mutant Ninja Turtles Exposed!   —Joan Hake Robie
(trade paper) ISBN 0914984314 **$5.95**

The Truth About Dungeons & Dragons   —Joan Hake Robie
(trade paper) ISBN 0914984373 **$5.95**
(cassette tape) ISBN 091498425X **$7.95**

What To Do When The Bill Collector Calls!
Know Your Rights   —David L. Kelcher, Jr.
(trade paper) ISBN 0914984322 **$9.95**

The Quick Job Hunt Guide   —Robert D. Seidle
(trade paper) ISBN 0914984357 **$7.95**

Man And Wife For Life   —Joseph Kanzlemar, Ed.D.
(trade paper) ISBN 0914984233 **$7.95**

A Candle In Darkness (novel   —June Livesay
(trade paper) ISBN 0914984225 **$8.95**

Horror And Violence—The Deadly Duo In The Media   —Phillips & Robie
(trade paper) ISBN 0914984160 **$8.95**

Turmoil In The Toy Box (1)   —Phil Phillips
(trade paper) ISBN 0914984047 **$8.95**

Turmoil In The Toy Box (video)   —Phil Phillips
(90 min. video tape—VHS only) 0006563589 **$34.95**

Turmoil In The Toy Box II —Joan Hake Robie
(trade paper) ISBN 0914984209 **$8.95**
(cassette tape) ISBN 0914984268 **$7.95**

Courting The King Of Terrors —Frank Carl
(trade paper) ISBN 0914984187 **$7.95**

Halloween And Satanism —Phillips & Robie
(trade paper) ISBN 091498411X **$8.95**

The Rock Report —Fletcher A. Brothers
(trade paper) ISBN 0914984136 **$6.95**

The Subtle Snare —Joan Hake Robie
(trade paper) ISBN 0914984128 **$8.95**

Inch by Inch . . . Is It a Cinch? —Phyllis Miller
(trade paper) ISBN 0914984152 **$8.95**

The Great Pretender —Rose Hall Warnke & Joan Hake Robie
(trade paper) ISBN 0914984039 **$8.95**

Devotion in Motion —Joan Hake Robie
(trade paper) ISBN 0914984004 **$4.95**

You Can Live In Divine Health —Joyce Boisseau
(trade paper) ISBN 0914984020 **$6.95**

To My Jewish Friends With Love —Christine Hyle
(booklet) 0006028098 **$1.00**

Purchasing Information